Rivers in the Rain Forest

Saviour Pirotta

RAINTREE
STECK-VAUGHN
PUBLISHERS
A Steck-Vaughn Company

Austin, Texas

Deep in the Rain Forest

PEOPLE in the Rain Forest

PREDATORS in the Rain Forest

RIVERS in the Rain Forest

TREES AND PLANTS in the Rain Forest

Cover picture: Children paddle their canoe in a flooded village in Brazil.

Title page: Boys having fun jumping in the Amazon River, during the annual flood in Amazonas State, Brazil

Contents page: The Rio Negro in Brazil during the rainy season

Published by Raintree Steck-Vaughn Publishers, an imprint of Steck-Vaughn Company

Printed in Italy. Bound in the United States.
1 2 3 4 5 6 7 8 9 0 03 02 01 00 99

Library of Congress Cataloging-in-Publication Data
Pirotta, Saviour.
Rivers in the rain forest / Saviour Pirotta.
  p.   cm.—(Deep in the rain forest)
Includes bibliographical references and index.
Summary: Introduces aspects of rivers in the rain forest including their plants and animals, the water cycle, flooding, and mining.
ISBN 0-8172-5138-3 (hard); 0-8172-8114-2 (soft)
1. Rivers—Juvenile literature.
2. Rain forests—Juvenile literature.
[1. Rivers. 2. Rain forests.]
I. Title. II. Series.
GB1203.8.P57 1999
551.48'3'09152—dc21   98-4587

Contents

Rain Forests Around the World

Rain forests are thick forests in parts of the world where there is lots of rain. Most rain forests are near the equator, an imaginary line that runs around the center of the earth. The largest rain forest is the Amazon, in South America.

◀ Mudskippers live in East and West Africa, India, Indonesia, and northern Australia.

◀ Gold can be found in rain forest rivers in Indonesia and the Amazon.

EQUATOR

◀ Carving canoes is an essential skill for people who live near rain forest rivers.

Rivers flow through every rain forest. The Amazon is the biggest river in the world. It flows through the Amazon rain forest. The Orinoco River cuts across rain forest in Colombia and Venezuela. The Congo River flows through rain forest in Central Africa.

◀ Tourists on a rain forest river trip up the Carrao River, in Venezuela

KEY

The green areas on the map show rain forests.

▲ Catfish are important food for people in the rain forest.

▲ Cows on rafts in a flooded village in the Amazon of Brazil

Rivers of Life

Rivers are essential to rain forests. They provide the forests with water all year round. Rivers also provide a home to many different plants and animals. People rely on the rivers, too.

▼ Clouds hang over the Manu River in Peru.

▲ People in rain forests are used to lots of heavy rain. This boy is using a palm leaf as an umbrella.

The water cycle

Water from rivers is always on the move. The hot sun heats the rivers and turns the water into a gas, called water vapor. The water vapor rises to the sky.

In the sky, the water vapor cools down.
It turns back into water and forms
clouds. When the water in the clouds
becomes too heavy, it falls as rain.

Some of the rainwater is used by the
trees and plants for growth. Other water
seeps back into the rivers. The journey of
water between the rivers, trees, and
clouds is called the water cycle.

▼ Rising mists and
clouds over rain
forest in Malaysia

The water cycle

2. The water vapor cools and forms clouds.

3. The water vapor turns back into liquid and falls as rain.

1. The sun heats the water in rivers and plants. It turns into vapor and rises in the air.

4. Rainwater seeps through the trees, flows back into the rivers, or goes underground.

River Plants

Mangrove trees grow in swamps, at the mouths of rain forest rivers. Mangroves have special long roots, which help anchor them in the mud.

Mangrove seeds sprout on the branches of their mother tree, instead of in the ground. This protects them from being washed away by the tide before they can grow into saplings.

▲ Mangrove seeds sprouting on their mother tree

▼ The roots of
mangrove trees
in Belize

Giant water lilies grow in rain forest
rivers. Some grow big enough for a
small child to sit on.

Victoria water
lilies grow in
shallow water.
Some can grow up
to 6 feet (2 m)
wide.

▲ Victoria water
lilies in the Amazon

Animals in Rivers

The rivers of the rain forest are home to many different fish, amphibians, reptiles, and mammals.

The mudskipper lives in the mangroves. It is a fish, but it can also breathe out of water. Mudskippers use their fins to walk as well as swim.

▼ Two male mudskippers look at each other angrily, with their fins raised.

Basilisks are amphibians. They are also called Jesus lizards because they can walk on water!

Basilisks have long webbed toes on their back feet, which act as paddles. They can run across small streams on their back legs.

▲ A basilisk, or Jesus lizard, running across a stream.

13

Animals as food

There are over 2,400 kinds of fish in the Amazon. Catfish are among the largest. They can grow over 6 feet (2 m) long. Catfish are a very important food for people.

The manatee is the biggest animal in the Amazon River. Manatees move very slowly, feeding on grasses on the riverbed.

▲ A fisherman with a huge catfish he has just caught in the Manu River, Peru.

▼ Manatees hold their breath for up to 15 minutes when they swim underwater.

Flood!

Rivers in rain forests often burst their banks, and deep water covers the forest floor. Then fish can get to parts of the forest they cannot usually reach.

Arowana fish are known by local fishermen as "water monkeys," because they jump out of the water. They leap up to 6 feet (2 m) above the water to catch beetles, spiders, and even birds and bats.

Arowana fish have ▶ large mouths, so they can swallow animals as big as birds.

The tambaqui fish particularly likes the seeds of the January palm tree. It can reach them only when the forest floor is flooded. The tambaqui cracks the seeds with its big flat teeth.

▲ Two tambaqui fish swimming up to a January palm to eat its seeds

People and floods

Most people in rain forests are used to the floods. Some people build their houses on stilts. Others build houses like boats, which float on the water when the rivers flood.

▼ Houses on stilts in the Amazon, surrounded by flooded forest

▲ Cattle graze on rafts during the yearly flood of the Amazon, in Brazil

When the water level rises, some farmers put their animals on rafts tied to the riverbank. The animals have to be careful not to fall in the water, where hungry piranhas could get them!

19

River Roads

Many rain forest people use the rivers to get around. It is easier to travel on the rivers than to fight through thick forest.

▼ This man is using an ax to hollow out a canoe in Papua New Guinea.

 20

The smallest boats on the rivers are canoes. They are made by hollowing out tree trunks. Richer people sometimes have motors attached to their canoes.

Canoes are used to get to school, to go to riverside markets, and to go fishing.

▲ The only way to get around in this flooded village is by canoe.

Carrying goods

On giant rain forest rivers, big freighters carry rubber, beef, and mineral ore to busy ports. Smaller boats are used to carry animals, coffee beans, and bananas to riverside markets. Big logs are tied together to make huge rafts.

▼ Huge logs are towed down a river on a raft in the Amazon, Brazil.

▼ Canoes carry goods to a riverside market in Colombia.

Mining

People have made their fortunes by finding gold or diamonds in rain forest rivers.

Prospectors sift through the earth from riverbeds, looking for precious stones. They use special pans or dishes, which separate the stones from the sand.

◄ A prospector looking for gold in Indonesia

Mining causes a lot of damage to rivers. It disturbs the water at riverbanks, where fish and other animals come to drink.

Prospectors drop mercury into the water, to help separate the stones. Since mercury is poisonous, it kills fish and animals in the rivers. Mercury can poison people, too.

▼ These gold miners are disturbing the banks of the Sekonyer River in Indonesia by looking for gold.

Saving the rivers

Rivers are being polluted by mining. We need to save the rivers, so that people can enjoy them in the future.

Without causing harm, tourists can take trips down the rivers and find out all about rain forests. They also bring money into poor areas.

You can help by finding out as much as you can about rain forests. There might be something you can do.

▼ This part of the Amazon rain forest has been destroyed by gold miners.

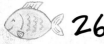

▼ Tourists on a river trip in Venezuela

Make a Rain Forest Canoe

YOU WILL NEED:

brown cardboard, or cardboard painted brown

tracing paper

a pencil

scissors

tape

Make your own miniature rain forest canoe by following these simple steps:

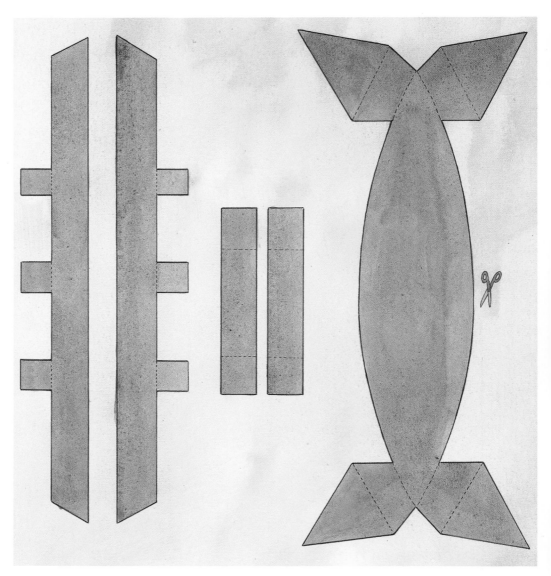

1. Trace the patterns on the right onto tracing paper and cut them out.

Then place the patterns on brown cardboard and cut out the patterns.

2. Fold up the ends of the canoe base, one after the other. Fasten the edges together with tape.

3. Add the sides of the canoe, putting them inside each end, and fasten them with tape on the bottom.

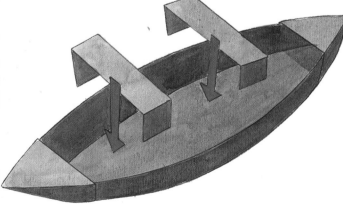

4. Now you can add the seats. Fold the edges of the seats and tape them to the inside of the canoe.

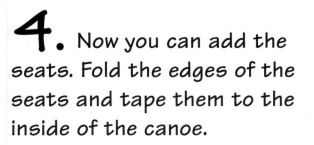

5. Now see if your canoe will float! You could have a race with a friend by blowing your canoes across a bathtub of water.

Glossary

Amphibians Animals that live on both land and in water.

Cycle A pattern of events that repeat themselves.

Freighter A big ship that carries goods, such as food or minerals.

Mangroves Tropical trees that grow in mud. They can survive when they are covered by seawater.

Mercury A poisonous liquid metal.

Mineral ore Rock with valuable metals inside.

Mouth (of a river) The part of the river where it meets the sea.

Prospectors People who look for minerals and precious stones in the ground, to sell for money.

Saplings Young trees.

Swamps Wet, marshy ground.

Tides The rise and fall of the surface of the sea.

Water vapor Water that has heated and turned into a gas.

Webbed Joined by a flap of skin as between toes or fingers.

30

Further Information

Other books to read

Cherry, Lynne. *The Great Kapok Tree: A Tale of the Amazon Rain Forest.* San Diego: Harcourt, Brace, Jovanovich, 1990.

Grupper, Jonathon. *Destination—Rain Forest: Rain Forest.* Washington, DC: National Geographic, 1997.

Harris, Nicholas. *Into the Rainforest: One Book Makes Hundreds of Pictures of Rainforest Life* (The Ecosystems Xplorer). Alexandria, VA: Time Life, 1996.

Lewington, Anna. *Atlas of the Rain Forests.* Austin, TX: Raintree Steck-Vaughn, 1997.

Nagda, Ann Whitehead. *Canopy Crossing: A Story of an Atlantic Rainforest.* Norwalk, CT: Soundprints Digital Audio, 1997.

Osborne, Mary Pope. *Afternoon on the Amazon.* (First Stepping Stone Books). New York: Random House, 1995.

CD Rom

Exploring Water Habitats (Wayland, 1997)

Useful addresses

All these groups provide material on rain forests for schools:

Earth Living Foundation
P.O. Box 188
Hesperus, CO 81326
(970) 385-5500

Friends of the Earth
1025 Vermont Avenue NW
Suite 300
Washington, D.C. 20005-6303
(202) 783-7400

Reforest the Earth
2218 Blossomwood Court NW
Olympia, WA 98502

The World Rainforest Movement
Chapel Row
Chadlington
Oxfordshire OX7 3NA
Tel: 01608 676691

World Wildlife Fund
1250 24th Street NW
P.O. Box 96555
Washington, D.C. 20077-7795

Picture acknowledgments
Bruce Coleman Ltd (Luiz Claudio Marigo) *cover, title page* , 21, (Jane Burton) 4 (top left), 12 , (Alain Compost) 4 (top right), 24, (Andrew Davies) 10 -11 (middle), Luiz Claudio Marigo) 19; Ecoscene (W. Lawler) 25; Robert Harding (K. Gillham) 22; NHPA (Martin Wendler) *contents page*, (Stephen Dalton) 13, (Jany Sauvanet) 26; Oxford Scientific Films (Michael Pitts) 4 (bottom), 20, (Harold Taylor Abipp) 8, (Max Gibbs) 16, (Nick Gordon) 17 (right); Panos Pictures (Jeremy Horner) 23; Planet Earth Pictures (Andrew Bartachi) 14; South American Pictures (Tony Morrison) 10 (left), 18; Still Pictures (Adi-Unep) 7 (top); Tony Stone Images (Kevin Schafer) 5 (top), 27, (Frans Lanting) 5 (bottom left), (Stuart Westmorland) 5 (bottom right), 15, (Frans Lanting) 6-7 (bottom); Wayland Picture library 11 (right). Border and folio artwork: Kate Davenport. World map and water-cycle artwork: Peter Bull.

Index

Page numbers in **bold** show there is a picture on the page as well as information.